God Moments

Volume I

30 Daily Devotions
to Awaken and Grow Your Faith

WENDY ADDISON

OLDE CROW PUBLISHING

God Moments – Volume 1
30 Daily Devotions to Awaken and Grow Your Faith

© 2024 by Wendy Addison

Scripture quotations marked (ESV) are from The ESV® Bible (The Holy Bible, English Standard Version®), © 2001 by Crossway, a publishing ministry of Good News Publishers. Used by permission. All rights reserved

Scripture quotations marked (NASB) are taken from the (NASB®) New American Standard Bible®, Copyright © 1960, 1971, 1977, 1995, 2020 by The Lockman Foundation. Used by permission. All rights reserved. www.lockman.org

Scripture quotations marked (NIV) are taken from the Holy Bible, New International Version®, NIV®. Copyright © 1973, 1978, 1984, 2011 by Biblica, Inc.™ Used by permission of Zondervan. All rights reserved worldwide. www.zondervan.com The "NIV" and "New International Version" are trademarks registered in the United States Patent and Trademark Office by Biblica, Inc.™

Scripture quotations marked (NLT) are taken from the *Holy Bible*, New Living Translation, copyright ©1996, 2004, 2015 by Tyndale House Foundation. Used by permission of Tyndale House Publishers, Carol Stream, Illinois 60188. All rights reserved.

Published in Ontario, Canada by Olde Crow Publishing.

ISBN: 978-1-990081-12-5 (paperback edition)
ISBN: 978-1-990081-11-8 (e-book)

God Moments

Volume I

Introduction

Welcome to volume one of my new *God Moments* devotional series. I'm thrilled to share these devotions with you in book format!

Thanks to your heartfelt feedback, what began as a devotional section in my author newsletter has evolved into something much more meaningful. Many of you shared how these messages have enriched and challenged your faith, and your requests for a book have inspired this series.

I invite you to pause and deeply engage with the scriptures and reflections in each devotion. These are not meant to be just another item checked to check off your to-do list but rather an opportunity to slow down, assess your faith, and deepen your relationship with Jesus. My prayer is that these moments will inspire spiritual growth and more intimacy with God.

At the end of each devotion, you'll find questions designed to prompt reflection and connection with the day's message. Take a moment to breathe deeply and immerse yourself in this exercise. God has incredible things to reveal to you. But if you're uncertain you're truly hearing His voice, always align it with scripture. God's Word is a steadfast guide, and through practice, persistence, and prayer, you will grow attuned to the Holy Spirit.

Remember, God desires a close and personal relationship with you. He loves you deeply and calls you His own. Don't lose heart; keep seeking, and let this devotional journey draw you nearer to His presence.

Wendy.

Day 1

$\mathbf{A}$ week or so after he started visiting our yard, Mr. Barred Owl met a terrible fate. We found him on our trail, having died shortly before we got there. Not gonna lie—I cried. I have a soft spot in my heart for birds.

I called it in because he had no markings to suggest why he died, and I wasn't sure if he needed to be tested for disease.

But he didn't. Apparently, he died of starvation, which can be expected for owls at certain times of the year.

That made me even sadder. I had no idea owls could have a hard time finding food! Had I known he was starving, I would have thrown him some raw chicken or something. I don't know if he would have accepted it, but I would have tried.

Losing Mr. Owl was just one unfortunate twist in a week that had spiralled out of control.

Add in an abundance of other mishaps happening at the time—the drama of three (almost four) teenagers, school, aging parents, covid and restrictions, and... phew! I felt like I was in a tornado.

Have you ever had weeks or seasons in your life like that?

Yet when everything is spinning, God is saying something:

Be still and know that I am God
(Psalm 46:10 – NIV)

Is your family life swirling out of control?
Be still and know that I am God.
Is your work overwhelming and causing you stress?
Be still and know that I am God.
Are the goings-on in the world threatening your peace of mind?
Be still.
Is life just too much to handle right now?
Know that I am God.
I encourage you, my friends, to grab a cup of tea and sit with God in the midst of all the turmoil. Be still. *Know* that He is God.

He's got you.

Reflections

What spoke to you the most from today's reading?

_____

_____

_____

_____

Turn your thoughts into a prayer:

_____

_____

_____

_____

Is the Holy Spirit prompting you to do anything in response?

_____

_____

_____

_____

Day 2

Have you ever completed a sugar fast? I've done it a few times, but occasionally, the fast isn't about diet or losing weight—and it isn't even about sugar.

It's about where I turn.

You see, the hunger inside us—the real hunger—is for God.

So, during the fast, I'm reminded that instead of turning to chocolate to get me through the tears, the irritation of a moment, or a bout of low energy, I'm to turn to God.

Instead of scrolling through social media to pass the time, distract myself from things, or avoid life, I'm to turn to God.

And instead of doing any of the things I usually do before turning to Jesus, I'm to go to Him first.

Because He is our living food. He is our portion. Our strength.

But those who hope in the Lord
will renew their strength.

They will soar on wings like eagles;
they will run and not grow weary,
they will walk and not be faint.
(Isaiah 40:31 – NIV)

I challenge you, my friend, to look at what you turn to this week. Where are your eyes focused? What do you look to? From what are you trying to draw strength?

And then I challenge you to turn to God instead. Perhaps you can fast for ten days from whatever is keeping you from Him.

Instead of giving into a habit or a craving, turn to Him and spend time in prayer, read the Bible, praise Him in song, or sit in His presence.

Only He can fill the void.

Reflections

What spoke to you the most from today's reading?

_____

_____

_____

_____

Turn your thoughts into a prayer:

_____

_____

_____

_____

Is the Holy Spirit prompting you to do anything in response?

_____

_____

_____

_____

Day 3

When I first brought Cookie Monster home, I felt like a mom to a newborn rather than a kitten.

I had to deal with having a litter box in my room (blech), morning goat milk feeding, afternoon wet food feeding, nighttime goat milk feeding, changing over dry food types and keeping the other cats away from the food.

Despite the zillion cat toys I left out for him, I had to stop him from chewing wires and build gates where needed.

I remember when he finally slept through the night while only occasionally walking across my face. However, I still slept lightly because I feared I might roll over onto him. He was so tiny!

But as with human babies, every moment was precious and worth it.

And isn't it that way with our relationship with God?

When we first come to Him, He's extra loving and tender as we muddle through the baby steps of our growth as Christians.

He gently guides us as we slowly learn what

isn't good for us and what our new boundaries should be.

He protects us and gates us off from things that could harm our new growth.

And He holds us as we sleep, staying up to watch over us.

What a beautiful picture of God's love! I'm so happy to call him "Daddy."

The Lord your God is with you, the Mighty Warrior who saves. He will take great delight in you; in his love he will no longer rebuke you, but will rejoice over you with singing.
(Zephaniah 3:17 – NIV)

What? God *delights* in us? Yes, my friend. God delights in *you*!

Of course, as we mature in our faith, we all must walk through challenges and trials.

But even then, He never leaves us.

He is the perfect parent. Never be embarrassed or afraid to sit in His lap and spend time with Him. He loves you more than you can imagine.

Reflections

What spoke to you the most from today's reading?

_____

_____

_____

_____

Turn your thoughts into a prayer:

_____

_____

_____

_____

Is the Holy Spirit prompting you to do anything in response?

_____

_____

_____

_____

Day 4

Over the last few years, I've learned a lot about computer and phone privacy. I've made adjustments and shifted to more secure programs and apps. Like most people, it's not that I have anything to hide (except maybe a few searches I've made for my murder mysteries that might be construed a different way) but it's the principle behind it.

Don't be fooled—your apps know everything about you: where you go, where you shop, what you buy, when you sleep, what you eat, and, ultimately, who you are. But no matter how much they know, they'll never know as much as God does about you.

For there is nothing hidden that will not be disclosed, and nothing concealed that will not be known or brought out into the open.
(Luke 8:17 – NIV)

One thing I've done is move my files to a more secure cloud. As I hit 'delete' to remove a large number of files and information from where they were previously stored, it occurred to me what a miraculous thing Jesus did when He died for our sins.

He hit 'delete.'

If we trust in Him, turn to Him, and follow Him, we can rest assured that we can face God with a blank, clean slate.

Isn't that good news?

Turn to Him today. There is nothing too big for Him.

Reflections

What spoke to you the most from today's reading?

_____

_____

_____

_____

Turn your thoughts into a prayer:

_____

_____

_____

_____

Is the Holy Spirit prompting you to do anything in response?

_____

_____

_____

_____

Day 5

It's no secret that I get super excited when autumn arrives. But that's not the case for everyone. I know a few people who feel down this time of year.

Instead of beautiful colours, they see plants dying.

Rather than enjoying the cooler weather, they're mourning the loss of summer.

And instead of seeing autumn as a step toward the cozy Christmas season, they dread the arrival of snow and winter.

For me, the opposite is true. In spring, I dread the mud and the damp weather. I get impatient waiting for the new growth and focus on the barren, leafless landscape no longer covered by a white blanket of beautiful snow.

And I start to stress about the too-hot days ahead.

Isn't that interesting?

While all the above feelings are certainly valid, especially for those who suffer from seasonal depression, it occurred to me that a lot of how we feel about life depends on how we look at it.

What glasses are you looking at life through? Are your lenses dismal and grey? Are they rose-coloured? Or are they God-lenses?

For we walk by faith, not by sight.
(2 Corinthians 5:7 – ESV)

Only God can give us the clarity to see things as He does, to find joy despite hardships, to keep going when times feel tough, and to praise Him in the good and the bad.

Faith sees us through, no matter what is in front of our eyes.

Let your faith guide you today. Keep your eyes on Jesus.

Reflections

What spoke to you the most from today's reading?

_____

_____

_____

_____

Turn your thoughts into a prayer:

_____

_____

_____

_____

Is the Holy Spirit prompting you to do anything in response?

_____

_____

_____

_____

Day 6

The same week my oldest child got her driver's licence, my son, who was fourteen years old at the time, had an issue with his shoes. His toes had begun to poke out of the end. A new pair of shoes was needed—and they were size eleven! What? He was only fourteen!

At the same time, his little sister was growing faster than I could keep up with. She went from size two to seven in less than a year.

It is easy to become overwhelmed by the speed of growth and change. It seems so out of control. We can't stop it, and it happens so quickly.

Whenever I turn around, someone is taller, bigger, or more mature.

But you know where automatic growth *doesn't* happen? In my walk with Christ. It's a growth that needs to be nurtured, watered, and treated with care. And if my faith was a plant, I've had months where it would be wilting.

Like newborn babies, you must crave pure

spiritual milk so that you will grow into a full experience of salvation. Cry out for this nourishment, now that you have had a taste of the Lord's kindness.
(1 Peter 2:2-3 – NLT)

It's so easy to be busy with life, work, family, and *things*. And it's so easy to let 'God time' slip to help provide more time for everything else.

But without God at the center, everything else is futile.

The good news is that God promises to always be there, waiting for us. He doesn't move. He is a solid rock.

Your relationship with Him will not wither and die like a plant and refuse to be revived. It is alive and, with a bit of care, always has the ability to flourish.

He's asking us to spend time with Him today. Answer His call. You'll never regret it.

Reflections

What spoke to you the most from today's reading?

_____

_____

_____

_____

Turn your thoughts into a prayer:

_____

_____

_____

_____

Is the Holy Spirit prompting you to do anything in response?

_____

_____

_____

_____

Day 7

This week, a friend of mine received a negative comment from someone. It got me thinking. Years ago, I wrote and produced a play. There were tons of good reviews and one negative one. Guess which one I remember?

Have you ever received negative comments? How about harsh words? Or even blatant insults?

I was severely bullied throughout my school years. Kids can be cruel. Unfortunately, with the state of today's world and the ease of using social media, adults can be cruel, too.

And what about people who are close to you? Have friends or family ever said anything harsh to you? Of course, they have.

It's inevitable. And words hurt.

So, what do we do? How do we handle it?

As always, the answer is: take it to God.

No matter what anyone says, *He* will always love you and me—unconditionally.

And I am convinced that nothing can ever separate us from God's love. Neither death

nor life, neither angels nor demons, neither our fears for today nor our worries about tomorrow—not even the powers of hell can separate us from God's love.
(Romans 8:38 – NLT)

He will never love you less because you have anxiety or depression.

He won't hold back His loving arms if you gain weight or eat the wrong thing one more time.

He will continue to love you with all His might when you lose your temper again or make another mistake.

He does not base His love on what you do, look, or act like.

He loves you because you are His. Nothing you do can make Him love you less.

Of course, this isn't a licence to sin whenever we feel like it, without consequence. But when we mess up and make mistakes, remember His love does not waver. We can easily pick up and start again.

Thank Him today. Relish in the fact that He loves you unconditionally. Rest in Him.

He loves you with all His heart.

Reflections

What spoke to you the most from today's reading?

_____

_____

_____

_____

Turn your thoughts into a prayer:

_____

_____

_____

_____

Is the Holy Spirit prompting you to do anything in response?

_____

_____

_____

_____

Day 8

While walking my pup on our trail in the backwoods one morning, I came across monstrous footprints. I'm accustomed to seeing dog prints, a few cat prints, and occasionally a deer or a fox print.

But these prints were huge.

My first thought was that they might be wolf prints. Or maybe even lynx. And then I quickly realized that they were nothing more than the previous day's dog prints, slowly melting and looking much more prominent than usual.

I sighed in relief, especially since we'd recently been walking the trail at night!

But it did get me thinking. Whether we mean to or not, we leave traces of us wherever we've been. Some things are apparent, like footprints, but others are not so obvious.

Like the hope we left in someone's heart when we encouraged them with prayer.

Or the morals and values we instill in our little ones as we raise them.

Or, on the unfortunate side, the hurt or pain

we've left with someone by using harsh words and our sharp tongues.

More than anything, I want to leave traces of my faith in God.

I want to leave His hope in others, His light in the darkness, His love in all I meet. Paul says this to Timothy:

I am reminded of your sincere faith, a faith that dwelt first in your grandmother Lois and your mother Eunice and now, I am sure, dwells in you as well.
(2 Timothy 1:5 – ESV)

While on this earth, we will continue to make mistakes and fall short of perfection, but how awesome would it be if, even amidst our shortcomings, we left a legacy of faith in our wake?

Let this be our daily goal.

Reflections

What spoke to you the most from today's reading?

_____

_____

_____

_____

Turn your thoughts into a prayer:

_____

_____

_____

_____

Is the Holy Spirit prompting you to do anything in response?

_____

_____

_____

_____

Day 9

For many years, we shared our property with a family of skunks.

Every year, proud Mama Skunk raises a few babies in a hole in the woods beside our walking trail.

One year, a couple of my kids and I saw some skunklets (if that's not the word for skunk babies, it should be). They skittered across the trail and dove into the hole right before us.

Before you freak out, have you ever seen a baby skunk? They're adorable! And they can't spray yet when they're little. At the time, we owned a large Goldendoodle. She walked the trails with me but never bothered with the skunk hole and usually listened well.

But then, one week, to my surprise, Mama Skunk made her way to the house and into our garage. I'd forgotten to close the door before coming in.

So, that evening, the dog got to go to the river for a walk instead of the usual house trail. Well, guess what the dog found at the river? Yup. A skunk. And she got sprayed!

So, that's the lesson in this today's God Moment:

Sometimes, no matter what you do, you can't escape the stink.

Dear brothers and sisters, when troubles of any kind come your way, consider it an opportunity for great joy. For you know that when your faith is tested, your endurance has a chance to grow. So let it grow, for when your endurance is fully developed, you will be perfect and complete, needing nothing.
(James 1:2-4 – NLT)

Sometimes, we need to go through things we don't want to. Sometimes, life is hard. We all have to face the stink at one time or another.

But as always, God is good. As always, He is there.

So, hang in there, my friend. Find joy in the process. God is working in you.

Reflections

What spoke to you the most from today's reading?

_____

_____

_____

_____

Turn your thoughts into a prayer:

_____

_____

_____

_____

Is the Holy Spirit prompting you to do anything in response?

_____

_____

_____

_____

Day 10

When my children were younger, they went on a ski trip with their dad, and I had the whole house to myself for a few days. It was strangely quiet, but I managed to be quite productive.

I used that time to repaint the entire upstairs open area, including the living room, kitchen, dining area and foyer. Whew!

Even though it's not my favourite task in the world, I love how painting covers the old and refreshes everything, making it clean and new.

Except it doesn't *really* do that, does it? It covers up the scratches and the old paint but doesn't replace it.

The old is still there, underneath, hidden—but existent.

Thankfully, our sin isn't like that.

When God forgives us as we accept Jesus as our Saviour, our sins aren't just covered up and hidden.

Our sins are *removed*.

They're gone—they're not under the old paint; the whole foundation is new.

We are clean and fresh in His eyes because He now sees us through Jesus.

He has removed our sins as far from us as the east is from the west.
(Psalm 103:12 – NLT)

They can't be any more removed than that, can they?

I hope this encourages you today. Don't look back—walk forward confidently in your freedom and forgiveness.

Reflections

What spoke to you the most from today's reading?

_____

_____

_____

_____

Turn your thoughts into a prayer:

_____

_____

_____

_____

Is the Holy Spirit prompting you to do anything in response?

_____

_____

_____

_____

Day 11

Certain birds resemble each other so closely that they are challenging to identify. Several flycatchers have only slight differences between them, and with two in particular, the only way to tell them apart is by their song.

They are the willow flycatcher and alder flycatcher. And even then, their song only has a bit of difference.

One time, before the days of apps and computer programs loaded with easy access to bird songs, I was birding with an experienced birder. We were extremely fortunate to come across a spot in the woods where the willowy shrubby habitat of the willow flycatcher butted up against the thicker, new-growth habitat of the alder flycatcher. And it was in that spot that we spotted and observed both species.

There is no better way to learn the songs than to hear them side by side. What a special treat that was! Yet, even in the presence of both birds, it still proved extremely difficult to separate them.

O Lord, you have examined my heart and know everything about me. You know when I sit down or stand up. You know my thoughts even when I'm far away.
(Psalm 139:1-2 – NLT)

Yet there is Someone who has no trouble separating our voices from each other. God the Father knows each and every one of us down to the most intricate detail. He never has to consult an app or look in a book to remember who is talking to Him. He instantly knows us—He even knows what is on our hearts and minds before we open our mouths and let Him hear our voices. There will never be a case of mistaken identity with God. He loves us profoundly and cherishes us.

He longs to hear your voice. Won't you talk to Him today?

Reflections

What spoke to you the most from today's reading?

_____

_____

_____

_____

Turn your thoughts into a prayer:

_____

_____

_____

_____

Is the Holy Spirit prompting you to do anything in response?

_____

_____

_____

_____

Day 12

The week I had major dental surgery was difficult. My weaknesses came to the forefront, and a reaction to the medicine escalated anxiety even more. It was rough going.

But God is good. He is always faithful. Although I know my suffering was nothing compared to what some people have gone through, I want to share what God showed me at that time.

We all go through suffering in our lifetime. The Bible says we will face all kinds of difficult things—whether it's a consequence of sin in the world or persecution for our faith—suffering is a promise. (What a great way to convince people to become Christians—LOL!)

But something else is also certain.

He will never leave us.

He will never forsake us.

Nothing can separate us from His love.

The Sunday following my surgery, I watched an online church, and the sermon was about pain and suffering. No coincidence about it—I love it when God does that!

The pastor told a story about how he hated getting needles when he was a child. He'd be worried for days, awaiting his appointment, stressing and dreading what was coming.

When it was time for the needle, the doctor reassured him it would only hurt for a second. Which it did—but he had been so focused on the pain and the worry of the pain it consumed him for days.

The pastor assured us that's what suffering is like—in light of all eternity, any suffering or persecution we face here on earth is a mere blip— a split second in the scheme of things.

I press on toward the goal to win the prize for which God has called me heavenward in Christ Jesus.
(Philippians 3:14 – NIV)

So, don't focus on the pain; focus on the *prize*.

And don't forget that all things work together for the glory of God.

Be encouraged, dear friend!

Reflections

What spoke to you the most from today's reading?

_____

_____

_____

_____

Turn your thoughts into a prayer:

_____

_____

_____

_____

Is the Holy Spirit prompting you to do anything in response?

_____

_____

_____

_____

Day 13

I love it when the autumn nights finally cool down enough that I can start wearing sweaters. In fact, I love the whole part of the year from September to December: back to school, autumn, Thanksgiving, the first snowfall, and Christmas!

And sweaters, and blankets, and tea... I love the feeling of a warm sweater with sleeves so long they cover half my hands. Add in a cozy quilt (and a book and a cat or two) and a cup of warm tea, and well—you might say it's my version of Heaven-on-earth.

Wearing a sweater on a cool day reminds me of what it feels like to be wrapped in God's love. For some people, it's the warmth of the sun on their skin that creates this feeling. For me, it's a soft sweater hugging my arms, akin to a bird protecting its young.

He will cover you with his feathers, and under his wings you will find refuge.
(Psalm 91:4 – NIV)

There is no place I'd rather be than under His wings, resting in the presence of my Heavenly Father.

I remember reading once about firefighters entering a newly burned-out forest and finding a charred bird. When they moved it, they found a live baby bird underneath its wings! What a picture of protection and sacrifice.

Just like Jesus did for us. He stretched His arms wide so the Father could wrap His around us. How beautiful is that? Rest in His arms today, my friend!

Reflections

What spoke to you the most from today's reading?

_____

_____

_____

_____

Turn your thoughts into a prayer:

_____

_____

_____

_____

Is the Holy Spirit prompting you to do anything in response?

_____

_____

_____

_____

Day 14

The evening before I was to have a new woodstove delivered, I read that the shipping policy only included curbside drop-off. From what I understood, the delivery person would leave the stove beside my driveway.

Immediately, I panicked. My driveway is over two hundred feet long! And I live out in the country where leaving something at the end of your driveway means it's free for anyone to take.

I quickly ran through a list of possible people I could call for help in the middle of the week. Did I need two guys? Three? Or my neighbour's tractor? What if that damaged the stove? And what if no one was available? Would I have to sit in my car beside the woodstove, guarding it until someone could help?

What if? What if? What if? I know by now that the "what if" questions are anxiety-inducing.

Can any one of you by worrying add a
single hour to your life?
(Matthew 6:27 – NIV)

And then I stopped my thought pattern. I prayed about it. I apologized to God for worrying, asked for forgiveness, asked Him to help me, and chose to leave it in His hands. I repeated this over and over until it stuck.

The next morning, a big truck rolled down my driveway. The delivery man wheeled the woodstove out on a dolly and readily obliged my request to put it in the garage.

Seriously? The delivery was that easy. That worry could have turned into a night of restless sleep and an anxiety attack.

I'm so glad I chose to give it to God instead. I know that doesn't mean things will always turn out the way I want them to, but it does mean I'm trusting God to help me every step of the way, no matter what happens. If I can do that every time I worry, it will go a long way to eliminating the anxiety in my life.

How about in yours?

Reflections

What spoke to you the most from today's reading?

_____

_____

_____

_____

Turn your thoughts into a prayer:

_____

_____

_____

_____

Is the Holy Spirit prompting you to do anything in response?

_____

_____

_____

_____

Day 15

All of my kids took their shot at archery. Yes, pun intended.

I recall sitting in on my youngest's first class. The teacher spent most of the time showing the kids all the equipment, reviewing the rules, and teaching them the proper stance.

Then she said something profound.

When the kids shot their set of three arrows, she said it didn't matter if they hit the bullseye. What mattered was that the arrows were together. Why?

Because consistency is essential.

As long as the three arrows were grouped, the kids were doing some things right. Their stance and form were good.

Aim comes last, with practice.

Isn't that a great analogy for our faith? Yes, we want to be like Jesus and do everything right, but we won't continually hit that bullseye.

For this very reason, make every effort to

add to your faith goodness; and to goodness, knowledge; and to knowledge, self-control; and to self-control, perseverance; and to perseverance, godliness; and to godliness, mutual affection; and to mutual affection, love. For if you possess these qualities in increasing measure, they will keep you from being ineffective and unproductive in your knowledge of our Lord Jesus Christ. But whoever does not have them is nearsighted and blind, forgetting that they have been cleansed from their past sins.
(2 Peter 1:5-9 – NIV)

What matters is the consistency. Our form. Our growth. Our persistence.

It's okay if we miss the mark.

God's guiding our process. Teaching us and grooming us.

Don't focus on trying to be perfect.

Just focus on Him.

Reflections

What spoke to you the most from today's reading?

_____

_____

_____

_____

Turn your thoughts into a prayer:

_____

_____

_____

_____

Is the Holy Spirit prompting you to do anything in response?

_____

_____

_____

_____

Day 16

As often happens while working at my desk, one of my kitties hopped up to say 'hello.' In this case, it was Holly. Since she's the most anti-social of my cat brood, I put up with her walking on my desk more than the others (okay, maybe that's not true—I put up with all of them because they're so cute and cuddly).

After allowing her to walk back and forth in front of my laptop 346 times while I pet her, she headed over to my little collection of fake succulents (you're about to find out why I have fake ones).

She gnawed on the tallest plant, and I cringed at the squeaky noise.

I promptly told her, "No!" and pushed her away.

And being a cat, she listened and went on her way—right?

As if!

No, being a cat, Holly marched back to the plant and chewed on it some more. I repeated the 'no' command and pushed her away for a second time. And then she once again ignored me and returned to the plant.

We repeated the process over and over and over again, several times!

Finally, she gave up, only to move on to my decorative mushrooms. From there, we repeated the chew, scold, ignore, and chew process all over again.

And that's when I knew this was a picture of persistence.

Who is more persistent than a cat trying to get their way?

And this is how we should be about our faith.

Persistent.

I press on toward the goal to win the prize for which God has called me heavenward in Christ Jesus.
(Philippians 3:14 – NIV)

Press on. Keep going. Work toward the goal.

Whatever you're going through—don't give up! Lean on Jesus.

Reflections

What spoke to you the most from today's reading?

_____

_____

_____

_____

Turn your thoughts into a prayer:

_____

_____

_____

_____

Is the Holy Spirit prompting you to do anything in response?

_____

_____

_____

_____

Day 17

After attending a friend's funeral, I spent some time thinking about loss. Losing loved ones is horrible, but it's not the only loss we experience.

There's another common kind of loss—a self-inflicted kind.

The kind that has to do with expectations.

Years ago, I learned to let go of high expectations (mostly), but I still have expectations in general—for my life, for my children, and for my career.

Surely, wanting my children to follow Christ or my books to change hearts aren't wrong expectations, are they? They're all in line with His will, right?

Of course, they are.

But it might not be God's plan—or at least not in the timing or way I expect.

And so, when my expectations don't come to pass when or how I thought they would, I suffer a great loss. A loss that then makes me ask things like, "Why, God?" and could even make me question my faith.

The heart of man plans his way, but the Lord establishes his steps.
(Proverbs 16:9 – ESV)

But let's take a look at that again. What's the common word in the above paragraphs? *My* marriage, *my* children, *my* career, *my* expectations.

Yup, I've made it all about me.

So, I've had to make a shift in the way I think. I *know* that my children, my career, my *everything* belongs to Him, but I'm not sure I've fully acted like it.

I've been trying to let go of all the expectations. Yes, I will keep praying and hoping for things that align with His will, but I will trust God to do what He wants in His timing.

I will do my best to focus on one day at a time, seeking to do what He asks of me.

Why don't you join me on this journey?

Reflections

What spoke to you the most from today's reading?

_____

_____

_____

_____

Turn your thoughts into a prayer:

_____

_____

_____

_____

Is the Holy Spirit prompting you to do anything in response?

_____

_____

_____

_____

Day 18

For years, my bedroom was also my office. Therefore, it was decorated with bookshelves and fairy lights everywhere.

The lights were all hooked up to a switch beside my nightstand. With one click, my room came to life.

Unfortunately, to make that work, there was a massive tangle of wires and extension cords under the bed. I'm sure it must have been a fire hazard of some kind.

So, one day, I decided to tackle the big, tangled mess.

I confess it took a while. I carefully unplugged each wire, untangled any knots, and coiled each cable with a twist tie.

As I put things back together (and eliminated some extension cords in the process), I realized that this 'mess' looked like my life before God got a hold of me. Twists, turns, knots and unnecessary baggage at every corner.

Did God just grab the mess and pull it apart? No! He gently worked on one cord at a time and sorted things out.

I might not be fully put back together yet, but one day, in Heaven, I will be! And so will you.

In the meantime, I'm grateful for God's tender care as he undoes the knots to make us better people. Some knots are tighter than others and need more work, but that's okay.

He won't ever give up on us.

We just have to be willing to let Him tackle the mess.

Therefore, if anyone is in Christ, he is a new creation. The old has passed away; behold, the new has come.
(2 Corinthians 5:17 – ESV)

Hand Him your tangled life today.

Reflections

What spoke to you the most from today's reading?

_____

_____

_____

_____

Turn your thoughts into a prayer:

_____

_____

_____

_____

Is the Holy Spirit prompting you to do anything in response?

_____

_____

_____

_____

Day 19

A couple of weeks ago, as I walked Ryley down the road, we passed the row of beautiful maples lining my neighbour's property. That's when I noticed one of the trees was full of dead leaves.

It was too early for the leaves to have changed for autumn, so I immediately realized that the tree was dying. It saddened me because it was so huge and beautiful.

But on the return trip, I took a better look and realized that it wasn't the tree, after all—but the branches of a massive vine that had grown to cover most of the tree over summer.

And it was dead because my neighbour had cut it from the root at the bottom.

Just one snip and all the branches lost their source of food and life.

I am the vine; you are the branches. If you remain in me and I in you, you will bear much fruit; apart from me you can do nothing.
(John 15:5 – NIV)

I don't think it's any coincidence that Jesus calls himself the vine. He is the source. He is the life. It's the perfect picture.

If we don't remain in Him, we become like that vast, dead branch covering the tree. It was big and ominous, but it was nothing but a pile of dead leaves without the root.

Remain in Him, my friends. Stay plugged into the root of the vine. Read the Word and spend time with Him every day.

He is our life source.

Reflections

What spoke to you the most from today's reading?

_____

_____

_____

_____

Turn your thoughts into a prayer:

_____

_____

_____

_____

Is the Holy Spirit prompting you to do anything in response?

_____

_____

_____

_____

Day 20

I once ordered new eyeglasses online. I wasn't sure how they would look once I received them, but I had no doubt they would work fine.

Why? Because ordering online is quite the process.

Not only do you have to enter the exact prescription numbers when you order, but you also need to measure the distance between your pupils to ensure the glasses line up correctly with your eyes for the best clarity.

Not something I would have thought of on my own. But it's so important!

Ultimately, you could have the right prescription, but if it's not properly aligned with your eyes, it will still cause problems.

You won't be able to focus.

This made me think—have I been aligned with God's word? Have I been studying, absorbing, and praying the scriptures? Have I kept God as my focus amidst all the chaos in my world?

Unfortunately, I realized I'd let some of my 'God time' slip away the previous two weeks. No wonder other thoughts had been overwhelming me!

Set your minds on things above, not on earthly things.
(Colossians 3:2 – NIV)

It doesn't matter how much is going on, how busy you are, or how little time you have.

If God isn't your focus, something else will be. And from my experience, that's not a good way to live.

Make today a good day by putting on your 'God glasses' and focusing on Him.

Reflections

What spoke to you the most from today's reading?

_____

_____

_____

_____

Turn your thoughts into a prayer:

_____

_____

_____

_____

Is the Holy Spirit prompting you to do anything in response?

_____

_____

_____

_____

Day 21

When I was a child, my parents owned a small strawberry farm. Every year, they plowed a new area to grow the farm and spent the summer preparing the field for the following season.

Without fail, every spring, killdeer would build nests among the rocky parts of the new fields. If I was patient enough, I could watch the kildeer from a distance and, as long as I didn't take my eye off the spot for even a second, I could find their nests with eggs so cleverly disguised that they looked just like other pebbles in the field.

Of course, every time I got near a nest, the killdeer would hop helplessly in the other direction and feign a broken wing. Such a clever deception to protect their little ones. Any predator looking for eggs for dinner would immediately be distracted by the easy prey of a larger, meatier bird with a broken wing.

Slowly, she'd lure the dangerous creature away from her eggs and towards herself. Then, at the last possible minute, she'd fly away, leaving both herself and her brood safe.

For I am convinced that neither death nor life, neither angels nor demons, neither the present nor the future, nor any powers, neither height nor depth, nor anything else in all creation, will be able to separate us from the love of God that is in Christ Jesus our Lord.
(Romans 8:38-39 – NIV)

I rest in the comfort of realizing that God also works like that. He protects us from the enemy. He went to all lengths to protect those He loves. He stretched His arms wide to save us. Let us rest in those arms that are never too weary to protect us.

Reflections

What spoke to you the most from today's reading?

_____

_____

_____

_____

Turn your thoughts into a prayer:

_____

_____

_____

_____

Is the Holy Spirit prompting you to do anything in response?

_____

_____

_____

_____

Day 22

Although it seems hard to recall now, training Ryley as a puppy was a lot of work.

I remember the endless times I'd show her the same thing over and over, teaching her how to behave, obey commands, relieve herself outside, and run free while keeping within the boundaries.

And how many times it felt like she would never get it.

Like, never ever.

But one day, while walking her along the trail, I suddenly realized how much better she'd been behaving.

She listened better, came when I called her, and pretty much figured out that outside is the place to 'do things.'

She learned what she was allowed to do and what she wasn't.

She now knows what she's permitted to eat and, for the most part, things she shouldn't eat.

Raising a puppy gave me a teensy bit of insight into what God must go through with us as we grow in our faith and stumble along in our spiritual journey.

Does He get frustrated with us?

Does He roll His eyes when we struggle to learn something and repeat the same mistakes again and again?

Somehow, I doubt it.

The Lord is compassionate and merciful, slow to get angry and filled with unfailing love.
(Psalm 103:8 – NLT)

He is patient. He is loving and full of mercy. He disciplines us with a soft, caring hand.

Isn't that incredible? I'm so thankful.

Be encouraged in your walk with Christ today.

Reflections

What spoke to you the most from today's reading?

_____

_____

_____

_____

Turn your thoughts into a prayer:

_____

_____

_____

_____

Is the Holy Spirit prompting you to do anything in response?

_____

_____

_____

_____

Day 23

One time when I went to the bakery to grab my essential ten-pack of large chocolate chip cookies, I noticed they had a new mini-pack of thirty.

I studied the packages briefly, trying to make the best decision. The 30-pack might last longer—I could eat a small one instead of a big one every time I wanted a snack.

On the other hand, it might be worse. I could end up eating more because they're so small.

After more contemplation, I got the 30-pack, figuring I had good self-control.

Uh… nope!

My youngest daughter entered my office just as I finished the last cookie (I keep them stashed in my desk).

"You ate thirty cookies?" Her eyes were as big as saucers.

I quickly reminded her how tiny the cookies were. In reality, both the 10-pack and the 30-pack contained the exact same amount of grams.

I also realized this can be about more than just cookies. Like prayer.

What's better? A longer, dedicated time in the morning where I can focus and savour my time with God? Or short little prayers throughout the day that help me consistently keep God on my mind?

I believe the answer is both!

Without setting aside time to spend with Him every day, the short prayers can become fleeting and less meaningful. Yet, if I were to spend time with Him only in the morning, I'd miss out on being in His presence throughout the day.

Pray without ceasing.
(Thessalonians 5:17 – ESV)

As in any relationship, it's essential to spend time with God. Sometimes, that means going deeper and having heart-to-heart conversations. Sometimes, it's finding joy in the little things. And sometimes, it's just about being in each other's presence.

In the end, what matters is that we're spending time together with God. Genuine relationships require it.

Reflections

What spoke to you the most from today's reading?

_____

_____

_____

_____

Turn your thoughts into a prayer:

_____

_____

_____

_____

Is the Holy Spirit prompting you to do anything in response?

_____

_____

_____

_____

Day 24

One chilly morning, while walking on a trail, I encountered a large puddle where the top layer had frozen into a sheet of clear glass. Underneath the surface, a few large air bubbles danced around to the movement of my feet.

The air had nowhere to go to escape.

And, as I do, I made a correlation between this and the Gospel.

The bubble reminded me of sin in our lives, trapped under the surface with no way to get rid of it.

Except one.

The One.

For God made Christ, who never sinned, to be the offering for our sin, so that we could be made right with God through Christ.
(2 Corinthians 5:21 – NLT)

Jesus is the only One who can break that

surface and release our sins because He is the only one who was righteous enough to die for our sins.

To take our place. Our punishment.

So, when you choose to ask Him into your life, to forgive your sins, and to follow Him, that ice shatters and the bubbles of sin vanish.

And that sheet of ice keeping you from God? It's no longer there. You have a direct line to Him.

Praise God. Praise Jesus for this!

Thank Him today for making a way for you to reach The Father.

And if you haven't reached out to Him, perhaps today is the day. He's waiting for you with His outstretched hand.

Reflections

What spoke to you the most from today's reading?

_____

_____

_____

_____

Turn your thoughts into a prayer:

_____

_____

_____

_____

Is the Holy Spirit prompting you to do anything in response?

_____

_____

_____

_____

Day 25

One day, I had a significant amount of work to do, but when I sat at my desk, I noticed suspicious charges on my credit card statement. I called the business, only to spend forty-five minutes finding out the charges weren't from them. Then I spent another forty-five minutes reporting to the bank that my credit card had been compromised.

After a quick lunch, I spent fifty minutes more on hold with the credit card company, followed by a twenty-minute conversation.

By the time I finished taking care of the situation, I had only half an hour before I had to pick up my daughters.

Needless to say, I felt frustrated! I followed this with thoughts like, "Why does this stuff always happen?" and "Why can't I just have a normal workday?"

I decided to walk to clear my head, and I remembered that frustrating things happen to everybody, every day, all the time.

What matters is how you react.

Unfortunately, I let the frustrations get the best

of me that day, and they robbed me of joy and peace. But it doesn't have to be that way.

Do not be anxious about anything, but in every situation, by prayer and petition, with thanksgiving, present your requests to God. And the peace of God, which transcends all understanding, will guard your hearts and your minds in Christ Jesus.
(Philippians 4:6-7 – NIV)

We all know people who continually let frustration get the best of them. They regularly complain about getting cut off in traffic, the rude cashier, or the glitch in a software program. Unfortunately, sometimes, that person is us.

The Bible talks a lot about not complaining and having a grateful heart instead.

And that is the answer.

No matter what, we should remain grateful to God in all things and through all things.

No matter what, He is in control.

Reflections

What spoke to you the most from today's reading?

_____

_____

_____

_____

Turn your thoughts into a prayer:

_____

_____

_____

_____

Is the Holy Spirit prompting you to do anything in response?

_____

_____

_____

_____

Day 26

Bzzz... bzzz... Can you hear it? The familiar buzzing of a hungry mosquito echoing in your ear?

One spring evening, after a grocery outing, our front door was left open a couple of inches. It was discovered after only a few minutes.

But guess how many mosquitoes found their way into the house in those few little minutes? Eleventy thousand and thirty-three. Yup. I counted each one as I squished them. I had the red slap marks on my arms and palms to prove it.

And for the next while, I waited, ready to pounce, anticipating the buzzing in my ear. And that's when I made the connection.

Do not conform to the pattern of this world, but be transformed by the renewing of your mind. Then you will be able to test and approve what God's will is—his good, pleasing and perfect will.
(Romans 12:2 – NIV)

The persistent, annoying mosquitoes reminded me of the doubts that had been creeping into my mind all week. It's so easy to listen to the negative voices until, before long, you're focused on nothing else. You wait for them, anticipate them, and heed them.

But, God asks us to think of what is noble, right, and pure.

I fully concede that focusing on the good, not the doubts and negative thoughts, takes effort.

But with God's help, we can do it. Arm yourself with His promises, especially with all the negativity in the world.

Reflections

What spoke to you the most from today's reading?

_____

_____

_____

_____

Turn your thoughts into a prayer:

_____

_____

_____

_____

Is the Holy Spirit prompting you to do anything in response?

_____

_____

_____

_____

Day 27

Do you know the expression, "All roads lead to Rome?" The Romans were the first to build a sound road system, so naturally, all the roads led to Rome. It helped boost their trade and made Rome 'the center of the earth.'

Life's not like that nowadays, is it?

Today, signs point in every direction, and you have to really think about which way you're headed—and I don't just mean road signs.

Things constantly scream for our attention... social media, streaming services, work, entertainment—you name it, it's calling your name.

It's so easy to become overwhelmed, distracted, and confused.

God is not a God of disorder but of peace.
(1 Corinthians 14:33 – NLT)

When you feel like you're being pulled in every

direction, remember that you're not alone. Take a moment to turn to Him. Let His wisdom and guidance be your compass in this chaotic world.

And then follow Him.

Sometimes, this means stopping what you're doing several times throughout the day and taking time to focus on Him. I'm continually working on this, and God knows I often forget to check His 'map.' But what I do know is that when I take those moments to ask Him where I should go or what I should do, He answers. And when I follow Him, the road is laid out for me.

And He will do the same for you. It doesn't mean there won't be bumps and potholes but know He is there with you for the ride.

Reflections

What spoke to you the most from today's reading?

_____

_____

_____

_____

Turn your thoughts into a prayer:

_____

_____

_____

_____

Is the Holy Spirit prompting you to do anything in response?

_____

_____

_____

_____

Day 28

I used a riding mower a couple of times as a teen, but it scared me, so after driving it into a bush, my dad gave up the idea of me cutting the lawn.

In my first home, I got stuck halfway up an incline. Thankfully, my neighbour ran over to help (and didn't laugh at me). That was the end of my lawnmowing exploits, until twenty years later, when lawn care became entirely up to me. You can guess I wasn't too excited.

It was scary the first time I hopped back on a riding mower, and driving under branches and getting sticks (and probably bugs) in my hair didn't encourage me to enjoy the job. The second time was better, and I got the hang of it by the third. Now, I almost enjoy it.

Next came the push mowing, to get to the areas unreachable with the riding mower. I bought a cute, easy-to-use battery mower that did a great job tidying up the out-of-the-way spots.

For the final touch, a weed trimmer does the job. I'm still working up the courage to use it. For now, my son helps.

Isn't this a great picture of our walk with God? First, He helps us tidy up the main areas of our lives—the ones most see as they walk by. And then, after a while, He asks us to look at the shadier areas. The ones you need to stop and look at to find.

So let us stop going over the basic teachings about Christ again and again. Let us go on instead and become mature in our understanding. Surely we don't need to start again with the fundamental importance of repenting from evil deeds and placing our faith in God.
(Hebrews 6:1 – NLT)

And then, of course, there's the trimming. Fine-tuning the edges and taking care of the final weeds. It feels scary, but He's not intrusive and waits for you to ask to invite Him into the darker spaces.

But He's waiting, and there's nothing to be afraid of.

Will you go deeper with Him today?

Reflections

What spoke to you the most from today's reading?

_____

_____

_____

_____

Turn your thoughts into a prayer:

_____

_____

_____

_____

Is the Holy Spirit prompting you to do anything in response?

_____

_____

_____

_____

Day 29

The day before my two oldest daughters' prom, I took all three of my girls to get pedicures. It was wonderful to have a special time like that with my girls, and our toes were so pretty.

Except, a couple of days later, my youngest developed a toe infection. The nail was green, and I don't do well with gross things. But thankfully, after a couple of days of treatment, it cleared up nicely.

And then, my daughter said I should write a God Moment about how her toe infection is like our hearts when we allow bad messages from Satan to get in.

Smart girl!

And so true. It's so easy to think of Satan as the creepy horned ogre who does horribly vile and wicked things. He *does*, but it's like the frog in the boiling pot analogy.

None of us would directly jump into disgusting, horrible sin.

In the beginning, Satan entices us with things that look appealing.

Like that show we watched, which didn't seem so bad initially but slowly got worse with each episode. Yet now we're hooked on the characters and make excuses to keep watching even if we know we shouldn't.

And before you know it... heart infection.

Or that time we tried something that seemed harmless, but over time, it's turned into an addiction, and now we can't seem to stop.

Heart infection.

So, what do we do about it?

He has removed our sins as far from us as the east is from the west.
(Psalm 103:12 – NLT)

Repent. Turn to God. Ask for forgiveness, and turn away from sin (which may require additional outside help if there is an addiction).

Then, we can rest assured that the 'infection' has been removed and our slate is clean.

Reflections

What spoke to you the most from today's reading?

_____

_____

_____

_____

Turn your thoughts into a prayer:

_____

_____

_____

_____

Is the Holy Spirit prompting you to do anything in response?

_____

_____

_____

_____

Day 30

One autumn night, I had just finished reading on the sofa in front of the fireplace and proceeded with my regular nighttime routine of turning off lights and locking doors. With only the dishwasher running in the background, it was peaceful and still.

Until I opened the patio door to unplug our outdoor fence lights.

A blast of wind hit me in the face and nearly made me lose my footing! The trees swayed like crazy, and the wind howled through the woods. Leftover leaves and other debris swirled around the yard.

Wow! I had no idea this had been going on outside! The dishwasher had muffled the sound of the storm.

The conditions were very different inside and outside the house.

And instantly, I was reminded of how God is our shelter.

The storms can rage, blow, and even cause destruction—but He is our refuge.

You have been a refuge for the poor, a refuge for the needy in their distress, a shelter from the storm and a shade from the heat.
(Isaiah 25:4 – NIV)

Crazy storms are going on out in the world today. Don't let them distract you from His presence. Run to Him. Take refuge in Him.

Remember when Peter walked on water to get to Jesus? The second he took his eyes off the Lord, he began to sink.

And therein lies the key. Keep your eyes on Him. He's got you.

Reflections

What spoke to you the most from today's reading?

_____

_____

_____

_____

Turn your thoughts into a prayer:

_____

_____

_____

_____

Is the Holy Spirit prompting you to do anything in response?

_____

_____

_____

_____

HAVE TEA WITH ME!

Thanks for reading God Moments! I hope and pray this devotional drew you closer to God. I'd love to spend more time with you. Join me for tea?

Tea With Wendy is a newsletter I send out to friends where I share photos, life stories, a God Moment, book news and other fun stuff.

And when you sign up, you'll get a few FREE GIFTS!

I'd love to see you there. Sign up at: wendyaddison.com/tea-with-wendy

HELP AN AUTHOR OUT?

Could you spare a minute and please leave a review for *God Moments – Volume 1*? It's the best thing you can do for an author, next to buying the book.

It doesn't have to be long. Giving a rating and writing a simple sentence will do. And you can simply copy and paste the same review to other sites. No need to write a new one. Thanks so much!

Here are suggestions for where you could leave a review:

Goodreads

Bookbub

Amazon

Your favourite online retailer

READ OTHER BOOKS BY WENDY ADDISON:

DEVOTIONALS:

God Moments Sampler – 10 Devotions to Awaken and Grow Your Faith
(FREE at wendyaddison.com)

God Moments – Volume 2: 30 Devotions to Awaken and Grow Your Faith (COMING SOON)

FAITH AND FOILS COZY MYSTERY SERIES:

Fishers of Menace

Apple of My Die (FREE short e-story)

Ablazing Grace

Peril of the Bells

Faith, Rope, and Love

Pray Without Deceasing

ABOUT THE AUTHOR

Meet bestselling author Wendy Addison, the creative mind behind soul-stirring devotionals that weave together faith, humour, and heartfelt insights to awaken your faith and enrich your spiritual growth.

Wendy's faith-driven journey is marked by a profound commitment to living out Christ's teachings through both personal and professional pursuits. Over the years, she has worked in children and youth ministry, directed a Christian theatre company, volunteered with international outreach organizations, and led Bible study groups. Her mission work and birdwatching adventures have taken her to nearly twenty countries, enriching her appreciation for God's creation—though spiders remain a challenge.

Wendy now resides nestled amidst the whispering trees of her 26-acre Canadian woodland retreat. She has four wonderful children, a fluffy dog, and mischievous feline companions who are always ready to lend a paw—or distract her with their antics.

So, wrap yourself in a cozy blanket with a steaming mug of tea and dive into Wendy's devotionals for a meaningful time filled with inspiration and warmth.

Sign up for the *Tea With* Wendy for regular updates, stories and new God Moments from Wendy, at: wendyaddison.com/tea-with-wendy

FOLLOW WENDY:

BookBub: @WendyAddisonAuthor

Goodreads: Wendy Addison

Facebook: Wendy Addison – Author

Instagram: @wendyaddisonauthor

Web: wendyaddison.com

Made in the USA
Columbia, SC
14 November 2024

45995222R00069